# Shaggy's Cheesy Lunch

by Frances Ann Ladd

Illustrated by Duendes del Sur

D0888275

SCHOLASTIC INC.

New York   Toronto   London   Auckland   Sydney
Mexico City   New Delhi   Hong Kong   Buenos Aires

"Like, I want lunch!"
Shaggy said.
"Shall we go, Scoob?"

"What shape food
should we eat?"
asked Shaggy.
"Round or square?"
"Round!" said Scooby.
"Round it is,"
said Shaggy.

Shaggy and Scooby
went to the
Cheeseburger Shack.
"What will you have?"
asked the lady.
"It's so hard to choose,"
said Shaggy.
"We will start
with cheeseburgers."

"Hey, Scoob.
Watch this!"
Shaggy shoved most
of the cheeseburger
into his mouth.
Then he drank
a big cherry soda.
"I am still hungry.
What else should I eat?"

Shaggy asked the lady
for a cheese pizza.
Shaggy and Scooby
munched on the pizza.
"That was good.
But I am still hungry,"
Shaggy said.

"I have a hunch you want chocolate ice cream, too," said the lady. "Right!" said Scooby.

Shaggy's chin
had cheese and
chocolate all over it.
"Jeepers!
Like, I need to wash
my face!" said Shaggy.
Scooby started to help.
"No, Scooby!"

Too late!
Scooby washed
Shaggy's chin
Scooby-style!
He licked it!